D0859703

Late Georgian and Regency Silver

Judith Banister

COUNTRY LIFE COLLECTORS' GUIDES

Fluted tea caddy with bright-cut borders.
John Robins. 1796. Height 6 in. 16·4 oz.
Private collection.

Sixty Changing Years

Numbers in the margin refer to the page where an illustration may be found

'Late Georgian' and 'Regency' are convenient, if not strictly accurate, terms used to describe silver made between about 1770 and 1830. The habit of classifying silver styles by the monarch on the throne dies hard – and it is a curious coincidence that in fact a change of style often did come about with the accession of a new sovereign. However, George III's reign was a long one, from 1760 to 1820, overlapping the age of grandeur known as the Regency, which is usually stretched, for stylistic purposes, from 1800 until George IV's death in 1830.

There is ambiguity, too, in the use of the term 'Georgian'. Some collectors, eager to give a cachet to late silver, loosely call anything made before William IV's reign 'Georgian'. 1830 is itself a somewhat arbitrary date to mark the termination of the 'antique' period, but it has been generally accepted as the end of the age of entirely handmade silver and other wares, a suggestion not wholly true, as will be seen.

The unifying factor of the period from 1770 to 1830 is really much simpler than any dynastic connection. It is the period of strong classical influence, based not, as in Renaissance times, on Italian originals, but on the art and architecture of ancient Greece, with Rome, Egypt and Asia Minor added for good measure.

Of course any sixty years reveal inevitable and frequent changes in style. There is a world of difference between a **tea-caddy** with fluted angles and pretty bright-cut ornament and a gargantuan centrepiece of sculptured pomposity, or between a functionally simple wine funnel and a bell-hung silver-gilt rattle and teething coral. Yet all were typical examples of the jigsaw of styles that led the fashion, or followed lagging in its wake, during the reigns of Farmer George and his dilettante son, George, Prince of Wales.

The era started with a revolution in taste. The sinuous, often contorted and expensively showy themes of the Rococo were tired. Even by 1760 leading London silversmiths had been looking abroad for new ideas. Some had come up with rather French designs, making a liberal use of reed-and-tie borders, and bolder, more formal ornament as a relief from the asymmetry and movement of the Rococo. But Louis XV styles did not appeal to the arbiters of taste this time. The inspiration came from further afield and from time past.

For some years young men and older connoisseurs, back from their cultural Grand Tours, had been talking of the splendours of the ancient civilisations being unearthed in Greece, Italy and Asia Minor. Antiquities began to be added to the Italian pictures and French furniture brought back in the baggage trains of the travellers. The 'coffee-table books' of the period, enthusiastically subscribed to, were illustrated works on classical antiquities, and measured drawings of columns, pediments and other remains filled every up-and-coming artist's and architect's notebook.

One of the most enthusiastic and far-seeing of the students at the excavations was a young Scotsman, Robert Adam. With great pertinacity he recorded minute details of what he saw at Rome and Pompeii, Spalato and Herculaneum. Ambitious, he found his way into society and by 1758 was fast becoming the world's most fashionable architect. Ably supported by his three brothers, Adam had the gift of being able to translate the classical remains he had studied into buildings, interiors and even into the everyday requirements of his patrons, applying classical themes to carpets, fireplaces and furniture, for instance, such as Greece and Rome could never have known.

Adam was only one of the great body of enlightened – and commercially minded – craftsmen of the period who could see

Design for a wine cooler attributed to E. H. Baily, possibly after William Theed. From an album of drawings in the Victoria and Albert Museum, London.

a profitable future in the new classicism. Everything could be created in the new manner, yet in fact nothing was new at all. At his new works, mistakenly called 'Etruria', Wedgwood was copying Greek vases. Dignitaries sitting for their portraits were painted in classical draperies, John Baskerville's 'Roman' typeface appeared in the bookshops, and the silversmiths, the cabinet-makers and the soft furnishers alike eagerly applied classical forms and ornaments to everything they made. As Josiah Wedgwood wrote to his friend Bentley, 'we will . . . captivate them with the Elegance and simplicity of the Ancients.'

Needless to say, the excavators of classical sites could contribute little in the way of metalwares for the craftsmen to copy.

Bat's wing
fluting
(see 28)

Reeding
(see 34)

Piercing
and
beading
(see 32)

Vitruvian
scroll
and
beading
(see 49)

Paterae
(see 12)

Silversmiths 'inventing' in the classical manner were obliged to follow originals in pottery and stone, and to adapt decoration from carved pediments and columns, from tesserated pavements and from the plentiful Greek vases and urns of all periods that now came to light.

The major innovation in silver forms was the wholesale use of the urn. This was adopted for everything possible, from sugar vases and race cups to épergnes and soup tureens. It appeared as the finial for covers and as the central motif on candelabra, which of course derived from **classical columns**. On occasion, the tripod and triangular pedestal provided a closely classical base, but on the whole the practical-minded silversmiths recognised that four sturdy feet were far sounder supports for large tureens, épergnes and jugs full of hot water than the slender satyr's legs which, though elegant, were none too easy to clean. For objects that could not happily be based on the urn-shape, the **oval** held sway. If the plain oval seemed too uninspired, then the **boat-shape**, often curved three-dimensionally, was substituted.

Decorative themes, always easily recognisable, were legion. Fluting, both simple, rather flat flutes, and the splayed pattern known as **'bat's wing fluting'** were revived. Edge mounts were also formally simple, and **reeding** and **beading** – or pearling as it was then known – were almost exclusively used. Applied decorative castwork was also much in demand, especially for expensive silverwares, and superb chased scrollwork – based usually on the **Vitruvian scroll** – applied festoons, foliate scrolls, laurel wreaths, medallion heads, rams' heads and the flat round ornaments in low relief, often of formal flower form, known as **paterae**, were used with splendid effect. Almost all the motifs can be traced to classical originals, either architectural or on painted Attic vases.

Chasing and cast applied ornament are essentially expensive, and the lightness associated with Adam design – especially in his walls and ceilings – was very successfully brought out by the silversmith by engraving. Engraving had, during the Rococo period, been in abeyance other than for inscriptions on presentation pieces and for the crests and coats of arms which served both as the owner's identifying document and to sustain his pride as one entitled to bear arms. The introduction in about 1770 of a new engraving technique, aptly called bright-cut, allowed silversmiths to reproduce with great delicacy and effect the shallow festoons and ribbon-bows, the flowerheads and vase-shapes of fashionable ornament.

Another technical development of the period was **saw-piercing**. Previously casters, strainer spoons and baskets had been pierced out by chiselling the metal away. Now fine cut-work could be achieved with the piercing saw, a surer method which, however, still needed skill.

Regular vertical piercing could also now be done mechanically, for the factory silversmiths had developed the fly-press and were also offering a service of parts, supplying galleries for baskets, cruets and so on already pierced out. In the same way, stamped out candlestick parts were available for assembly as required, while business in the supply of wire and other mounts increased throughout the period.

A taste for simplicity came at an opportune moment for the development of the silver and allied industries in Birmingham and Sheffield. The 18th century had seen enormous developments in the industrial field. Factories and factory towns had spread over the Midlands with hideous effect. But the products of the machine were far from despised. The ever-increasing market of middle class customers was also growing richer. These people wanted the luxuries – or passable imitations of them – that the leaders of taste decreed were in the fashion. The silversmiths of the Midlands could, with the new formal styles, 'invent' a whole series of designs in silver, Sheffield plate and white metal to be made up with the help of their newly installed stamping machines, fly-presses and plating plant.

Everything, whether made by hand in the craftsman's workshop, or produced in quantity in provincial factories, followed the classical pattern to greater or lesser extent.

Alongside this industrial development came a change in shopping. Manufacturers sold their products to shopkeepers who now dealt chiefly as retailers and no longer made up their own wares. Some of the leading London retailers, as today, were able to keep subsidiary workshops fully occupied, though even they bought in certain wares, such as casters and cruets, candlesticks and so on, from specialist makers – a trend that had been growing throughout the century. And even those silversmiths who maintained the name of London as the centre of hand craftsmanship sometimes bought in silver from Birmingham and Sheffield makers – even overstamping their own silver mark over that of the provincial manufacturer.

During the Regency, which officially started in 1811, the rift between handmade and factory-made grew wider still. The first glimmerings of the grand manner came in the last decade of the 18th century. It can be claimed that the Prince of Wales was the moving spirit of the new grandeur. He had grown up in the heyday of the Adam movement. In 1783 he was given Carlton House as his own residence, an old house in a bad state of repair. The Prince engaged Henry Holland as his architect. Holland was a noted opponent of Adam's pretty, light approach to the classical. Within a year the Prince had had much of Carlton House transformed into a sumptuous mansion. Needless to say, he took no notice of the King's demands that he should merely repaint the house and put in some appropriate furniture. The men of taste, like Horace Walpole, approved of its 'august simplicity'. The Prince was setting a new style.

Carlton House whetted the Prince's appetite, and in Rundell & Bridge he found a firm of silversmiths and jewellers eager and able to execute his lavish orders. It is paradoxical that the King should himself have introduced his extravagant son to Rundell & Bridge. It was noted by George Fox in his memoirs of the firm that the King 'would almost command the Parties to go to Ludgate Hill for any Plate or Jewels they might want . . . and very many splendid orders were received in consequence.'

The Prince was not alone in promoting rich tastes in silver. The long drawn out Napoleonic wars and a grateful nation's rewards for service, in the form of ornamental plate, provided London silversmiths with plenty of orders for special pieces.

Lower down the scale other silversmiths catered in a less lavish manner, but still in the tradition of copying the most fashionable styles, for those who could not afford much ornamented silver. Some of it was well made, some notoriously flimsy. Indeed wise householders often chose sturdier Sheffield-plated wares than thin ones of silver. But basically the styles were the same, and the silversmiths were hard put to it to contrive the decorative details of high Regency silver at a price their customers could afford.

Perhaps it was this following of fashion that finally wrought such havoc among the 19th-century silversmiths. When the machine first helped to increase production in the later 18th century, styles were relatively simple. The Regency period saw the sculptor-designer dominate the silversmith's workshop, men who, no doubt in good faith, wanted to express their **grand designs** in the richest metals, but who had little or no experience of silversmithing. Watered down versions of such pomp and circumstance could only be banal.

Replica of the Warwick Vase.
Paul Storr. 1820. Height 9½ in.
The Worshipful Company of Goldsmiths, London.

Silver
for Display and
Lighting

The 18th century was rich in silver for decorative purposes. Two-handled cups, with or without covers, large vases, ewers and sideboard dishes made a brilliantly opulent show and carried on the tradition of the loving cup and the rosewater dish and ewer still in use at City and Livery functions, as Creevy recorded in his diary.

There was no lessening in the demand for decorative silver during the Adam period. Indeed the fashion for having Greek and Roman pots in one's collection, Chinese porcelain, hardstones mounted in ormolu, Wedgwood jasper and other stonewares no doubt also increased the demand for silver ornaments, while the national fervour for racing and other sports encouraged the presentation of more and more prizes and trophies, by now almost always in the form of cups.

After the contorted motifs and swirling forms of Rococo silver, the Neo-classical vases were formal and restrained. But they were far from plain, and the finest cups and covers of the 1770s were examples of highly skilled craftsmanship, with meticulous chasing, applied ornaments, cast figure finials and masks, small applied classical plaques and paterae. Some followed pottery or stoneware originals, such as the Wedgwood-style vase of 1772 in the Victoria and Albert Museum, with its alternate matted and plain vertical panels and ribboned drapes at the base and round the top of the egg-shaped bowl, and with cast satyr's masks on either side.

Lloyd's Patriotic Fund vase with
corded scroll handles enclosing paterae.
Vases on plinths were presented only
to admirals who fought at Trafalgar.
Benjamin Smith. 1808.
Height 26¼ in. 354·9 oz.
Formerly in the collection of the
Earl of Northesk.

Vase-shaped race cup and stand.
William Holmes and Nicholas Dumee. 1774.
Height 21¾ in. 244·5 oz.
City Art Gallery
(Temple Newsam House),
Leeds.

Racing cups, usually gilt, were also made in the new style.
12   Sometimes, as in the magnificent **cup and stand** of 1774 at Temple
Newsam, Leeds, the rich ornament seems to hark back to a sort
of formalised Rococo in its lavish treatment of classical motifs.

As the century grew older, cups tended to become more and
more formal, with high loop handles and high covers topped
with pinecone and acanthus-bud finials. Many were presenta-
tions to officers who distinguished themselves in sieges, battles
and marine encounters, and the bell-shaped bodies were decorated above the fluted or leaf-girt bases with applied medallions, trophies of arms and suitable inscriptions from grateful
commanders, underwriters and other dignitaries.

By 1800 cups and covers became grander again. The graceful
loop handles gradually disappeared in favour of twin scrolls,
as on a cup and cover given in 1799 as a christening gift by
George III, or became angular, as on the Doncaster Race Cup of
12   1801. Then in 1805 came the impressive series of **Trafalgar vases**,
designed by John Flaxman and made by Digby Scott and Benjamin Smith and their successors, until about 1810. The vases
were subscribed for and awarded by the Patriotic Fund at Lloyd's,
and were made in various sizes according to the seniority of the
admirals and captains who fought at Trafalgar. The sides were
applied with two scenes, one of Britannia holding a figure of
Victory, the other showing Hercules slaying the hydra. Scroll
handles enclosing rosettes rise level with the model of a lion on
the disc cover. Other vases, slightly varied in design, were also
made for other purposes, among them one for the Honourable
East India Company in 1805.

The commissioning of the sculptor John Flaxman to design the
Lloyd's vases presaged a new approach to the design of silver
cups and other objects, such as wine coolers, based on the vase
form. Nearly all the presentation trophies to generals and others
during the last years of the wars with France were grandiose,
and many featured elaborate cast figures – Greek caryatids,
angels, lions, elephants and so on. Similarly vast and far from
domestic treatment of silver is represented by the enormous
presentation candelabrum, standing 57 inches high, made by

Benjamin Smith in 1816 for presentation to the Duke of Wellington by the merchants and bankers of the City of London. It is now at Apsley House.

Such large candelabrum-centrepieces became even more fashionable in the 1820s, when the themes from Greek mythology were shown, not in applied relief, but in the round, as an enormous rocky sculpture in silver made by Edward Farrell in 1824 for the Duke of York, brother of George IV. It stands 35 inches high and weighs more than a thousand ounces. At the top Hercules is slaying the hydra, each of whose nine heads holds a candle-nozzle as it writhes above a rocky plinth.

'Massiveness, the principal characteristic of good Plate,' was a keynote of the work of Charles Heathcote Tatham, whose name appears as the designer of a series of large silver-gilt dishes formerly in the collection of the Marquess of Camden. Made by William Fountain in 1805, there are three circular sideboard dishes, one $27\frac{1}{2}$ inches in diameter, a pair $21\frac{1}{2}$ inches across. The centres are applied with the royal arms in high relief and surrounded by a trail of enormous leaf-shapes on the broad rims. And massiveness, too, was the theme of the sideboard dishes of the 1820s, at which silversmiths such as Edward Farrell excelled, just as Smith and Storr had done in the first two decades of the the century.

One of Storr's most frequently executed classical subjects was the **Warwick Vase**, copying in silver the antique vase now at Warwick castle. The vase is applied with eight classical masks and has intertwining handles. Its popularity as a subject of ornamental plate continued well into the 1820s, after Storr had left Rundell, Bridge & Rundell, and the vases were made by Philip Rundell. Variations of the Warwick Vase also exercised the ingenuity of other silver designers and silversmiths in the years after Waterloo, and various Roman marble originals were copied in silver both for ornamental vases and for table centres, wine coolers and dessert stands.

Such attention to opulence for its own sake was a far cry from the eminently **practical candlesticks** and **branched candelabra** of the 18th century. Even before the death of the Rococo, the

centre One of a pair of candelabra with fluted vase-shaped stem.
John Schofield. 1789. Height 17¾ in. 98·6 oz. Private collection.

Two from a set of four silver-gilt candlesticks with foliate low relief decoration.
John Schofield. 1791. Height 14 in. 196·5 oz. Private collection.

Chamber candlestick with
extinguisher.
John Schofield. 1789.
Private collection.

Adam design for a candlestick.
From volume 25 of Adam's drawings.
Sir John Soane's Museum, London.

One of a pair of
candlesticks, loaded.
J. Tibbits, Sheffield. 1775.
Private collection.
(Mark: see 62)

Guilloche
(see 53)

Gadrooning
(see 26)

Corinthian column had been adopted by silversmiths as a new style for candlesticks, and even in the 1770s some of the first truly **Neo-classical candlesticks** were not in the style immediately associated with Adam. Some were almost pompous, based on tapering classical pedestals of Roman rather than Greek inspiration, heavily overlaid with formal acanthus foliage, and with festooned shoulders and rams' or lions' mask knops. Rather angular terminals where the branches were fitted to the main stem added to the somewhat ponderous look.

However, there is a pair of candlesticks, based on **Adam's own drawings**, now in the Soane Museum. They date from as early as 1767 and are by John Carter, one of the leading London makers of candlesticks. Here the traditional baluster form of the English silver candlestick is adapted, given formality with a square base, and richness without Rococo ebullience by acanthus foliage borders, **guilloche** and beaded ornament, and acanthus foliage at the bases of the fluted stems.

The elongated baluster form was largely superseded about 1780 by the fluted style with V-shaped stem, which tapered to a broad band, often plain except for narrow beaded borders, below the vase-shaped sconce. Bases, almost always circular, were also plain, at most being stepped and decorated with beading, **gadrooning** or reeding, though gradually the fluting came to be extended from the well in the base to the base of the stem.

Many candlesticks were provided with branches, and the use

17

of these greatly increased towards the end of the century, until almost all styles were made as candelabra. The early branches were mostly of curved form, with a spiral encircling the top of the stem which was not infrequently capped with a vase-like finial. Simple reeded branches were, by the 1790s, often enriched with formal foliage and even, on occasion, with flower sprays in the Rococo manner.

By the end of the century the fashion for more elaborate silver introduced two new styles – a square-based columnar candlestick of the formal Napoleonic style, and the classical figure stem, holding aloft a torch-like candle-socket. Elaboration was further emphasised by gilding – which also had the advantage of making the cleaning of high relief ornament less onerous.

The search for new designs led some of the London silversmiths back into the past of English silver. Paul Storr in 1800 made, for Vulliamy's, the retailers, a pair of small candlesticks of 'Gothick' inspiration for the eccentric William Beckford of Fonthill. They have, indeed, what we might now call a Pre-Raphaelite quality. The fashion for Neo-Gothic was limited, but occasional specimens are found during the next fifteen years or so. A more usual, and to the ornament-loving patrons of the period, highly acceptable style for revival was the Rococo. From about 1807 onwards the true Regency styles, with their classically inspired motifs, were interspersed with Rococoisms, sometimes exactly copied or, apparently, even cast in the moulds that had been used in the 1740s.

Figure candlesticks of a Rococo rather than classical inspiration made a reappearance in the first decade of the century, with demi-figures and cherubs rising from rocky shell-encrusted bases. The true Regency style figure-candlestick was a far more formal and impressive affair. For the national heroes, such as Sir Arthur Wellesley, his officers would themselves appear in detailed models to support a stem formed as imperial fasces, while the base would have Roman-style bas-reliefs of warlike feats. In less martial vein the classical tripod candelabrum had a stem formed by a trio of Egyptian caryatids, bacchantes or lions' masks rising from tapered columns. In the strictest sense these too were designs

One of a pair of candelabra of tripod
form, showing Egyptian influence.
Benjamin and James Smith. 1808.
Height 29½ in. The pair 512·5 oz.
Private collection.

One of a pair of silver-gilt
seven-light candelabra, with figures
of Pan and nymphs at the base.
1814. Height 37 in. 522 oz.
The Worshipful Company of Goldsmiths,
London.

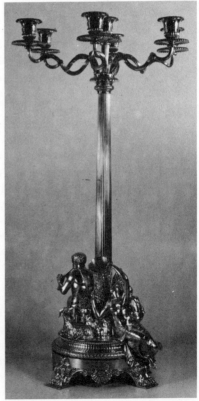

derived from war, for it appears that the Egyptian themes were brought to England following Napoleon's excavations in Egypt. By the time of Waterloo they were all the fashion in London: a 19 superb set of **two-branch candelabra**, with tapered cluster columns and Egyptian figure terminals, the scrolling branches with lotus and formal flowerheads, was made by Benjamin Smith in 1807 and graced the banqueting table in Brussels on the eve of the battle of Waterloo.

The candelabrum, with two, three, four, five or seven branches, gave the silversmith ample scope for almost scenic treatment, and in 1814 Paul Storr combined classical simplicity and legend in a 19 pair of **seven-light candelabra**, now in the Goldsmiths' Company collection. An elegantly simple fluted column carries simple scrolling branches for the fluted and gadrooned sconces, while the heavy circular paw-footed and shell-girt base supports a group of Pan playing his pipes with nymphs and goats beside him.

In less spectacular form the candlestick was formally chased with foliage, basketwork and honeysuckle motifs borrowed directly from classical originals, but the taste for elaboration in no way abated, and Rococo, classical and intricate compositions with sculptural affinities provided imposing centrepieces that achieved added effect by their also being candelabra. By the end of the period Rococo and the sculptured figure held sway, and it was left to the Sheffield makers to provide less florid silver candlesticks for everyday use, based on less exotic, but none-theless Rococo, forms.

Even the inkstand underwent a sculptural treatment, with Homer, Virgil and Milton supporting a figure of winged Victory for a royal gift made in 1821 by Philip Rundell, though the rectangular tray, by the 1820s with, of course, a rich Rococo border, showed the writer in more practical if less lyrical mood.

At the beginning of the Adam period, the fluted vase had supplied a fortunately classical shape without the necessity of much altering the basic form of the inkstand, though by the 1780s the boat-shape was generally preferred, either with a reeded everted rim or with a pierced galleried edge. A charming series of globe-shaped stands were made between about 1790 and 1805 by the London silversmith John Robins, no doubt for the band of young ladies endlessly busy, like Fanny Burney, with their diaries and memoirs. Standing on a domed foot, the globe is held in an open frame and a falling top conceals the miniature wells and other writing accessories inside.

21   Regency **inkstands** were grander, but often most attractive, with acanthus-overlaid pots and rich 'Egyptian' feet. Almost all the most elaborate inkstands were gilt and, as if to emphasise their splendour, even had silver mounted glass liners to the pots instead of the glass pots and plainer oblong trays of more moderately priced silver inkstands.

In addition, there were various other writing accoutrements including bells, also used as table bells, tapersticks, magnifying glasses, penknives and even quill pens.

Silver-gilt inkstand with central wafer box, taperstick and extinguisher. Philip Rundell. 1821. Private collection.

Dining-room Silver

23 Every summer visitors to the Royal Pavilion at Brighton have an opportunity to see just how magnificent a **nobleman's table** would have appeared at the time of the Regency. The tables of the Adam period were no less grand. Indeed the second half of the 18th century saw a tremendous variety in dining-table silver, with increasing use of matched sets of dishes, plates, tureens for soup and sauce, cruets, wine coolers, bottle stands, and table centrepieces.

Complete dinner services were often both large and splendid. Even soup and meat plates were included, often a pair of soup tureens, and sets of four or even eight sauce tureens, with equally large numbers of serving dishes, entrée dishes, vegetable dishes and so on. In addition there would be dessert plates, dishes, baskets and épergnes, often gilt, while flatware (spoons and forks) and cutlery (knives) would be provided in matching sets, again for dessert frequently gilt, and with silver instead of steel blades and richly wrought handles.

23 Adam themes were particularly suited to the **soup tureen,** for which the oval had long been the most functional and fashionable
23 shape. **Rams' mask handles**, acanthus and palmate foliage, swags of husks, wreaths of bay, oval medallions and formal flowerheads were extensively used, and many of the finest tureens – partly, no doubt, because the mask handles were not particularly efficient, and partly for greater splendour – were also provided with chased oval stands.

Adam-style soup tureen with
applied classical medallions.
Daniel Smith and Robert Sharp. 1777.
Length 14½ in. 110 oz.
Private collection.

The banqueting table in
the Royal Pavilion, Brighton.

23

The oval was also a suitable shape for fluted and half-fluted bodies, and fluting round the finial of the stepped covers became almost uniform on decorated tureens of the 1770s and 1780s. Probably the large size of the soup tureen, usually about 15 inches long, and the weight, which was usually between about 85 ounces and 150 ounces apiece, deterred all but the richest purchaser from having his tureens elaborately decorated. At all events the great majority of Adam period soup tureens are simple, their plain bodies relieved only by beaded, reeded or gadrooned edges, graceful high loop handles, usually reeded, and perhaps a finial in the form of the owner's crest, or of an urn or pinecone. By the 1790s the truly Adam style tureen, with delicate classical decoration chased with foliage and applied with foliate swags, was only made for special occasions, such as the presentation tureen of 1791 by John Schofield for the headmaster of Westminster school – in a style closely akin to the Adam designs in Matthew Boulton of Birmingham's early **pattern books**. More usually the soup was served from an oval, or sometimes circular, tureen with an oval foot, high loop handles, and the body half-fluted. Fluting was often exceptionally well done, following the curves of the body and cover, and often in the style known as bat's wing, which spreads out towards the open end.

But even the practical tureen underwent a change about 1800. The plain oval on its oval foot, sometimes supported on a square pedestal, became slightly bulbous, and stood on four sturdy foliate or paw feet, while the graceful loop handles were replaced by double loop handles capped with foliage, or by short side-handles emerging from a bed of foliage. More and more, finials were decorative versions of the owner's crest, or else reverted to Rococo styles with flowers, buds or fruit clusters.

For important tureens ornamental styles were inevitable, and they were enriched with applied cast and chased oak-leaves, scrolls, vine-leaves and grape clusters, paterae and lions' masks. Four cast feet appeared to be rather more popular than oval or circular bases, and the most magnificent tureens of the Regency period were, like their early Adam period forebears, supplied with elaborate oval stands. About 1810 the Rococo revival came

A page of
jug designs.
From
Matthew
Boulton's
first
pattern
book.
City
Reference
Library,
Birmingham.

Matthew
Boulton
(Birmingham,
1827)

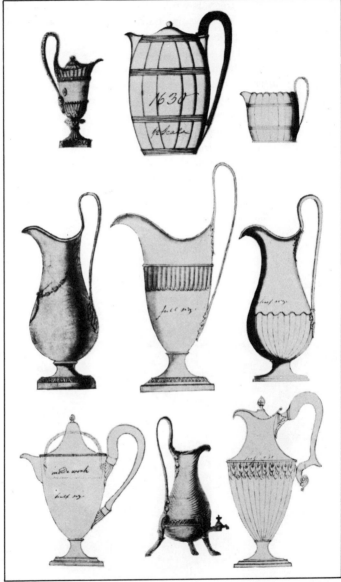

to the tureen as well as to other silver, and in 1812 Paul Storr made a superb pair of silver-gilt tureens and stands, weighing 1073 ounces, for the royal collection. Two years later Robert Garrard revived the 'quilted' style of decoration for a shaped oval tureen that might well have been made in the 1750s. But the years after Waterloo saw an unexpected **Baroque style** almost generally used for the tureen, with compressed half-fluted bodies, shell or leaf-encrusted handles springing from lions' masks, and equally richly decorated shaped handles on the domed covers, on which a band of gadrooning often matched the gadrooned rim and foot. The more ornate styles of the 1820s altered the basic style not at all, though now the four paw feet were overlaid with applied

Formal half-fluted and gadrooned soup tureen.
Philip Rundell. 1820. Width 12¼ in. 107·7 oz. Private collection.

cast foliage, often oak-leaf, which spread along the ends of the tureen towards the foliate end-handles, and at the base of the handle on the cover. The great masters of silver such as Storr, John Bridge and Edward Fernell tended, however, to hark back to Rococo fantasy, as in Storr's **triton-decked tureens** of 1820 and 1821, formerly in the Duke of Devonshire's collection, and the set of four shell tureens in the royal collection which John Bridge in 1826 adapted from his own earlier centrepieces of 1824. Their rich style became the basis for the lobed and fluted tureens, enriched with oak-branches and other scrolling foliage that ousted the plain silver tureen for years to come.

The design development of the sauce tureen exactly parallels

One of a pair of Rococo revival soup tureens and stands.
Paul Storr. 1820 and 1821. Width 21 in. The pair 1049 oz.
Formerly in the collection of the Duke of Devonshire.

that of the soup tureen. The changeover from sauce boat to sauce tureen was almost universal, though the early 1770s witnessed occasional efforts to create sauce boats in the Adam style, such as a rare pair of 1771 by Butty and Dumee, with boat-shaped bodies on an oval foot, and decorated with festoons falling from central masks and with ring handles. Already, though, here was the

28 **boat-shaped tureen** replacing the standard form of sauce boat, and soon covers became as inevitable as the oval form with its greater or lesser degree of Neo-classical decoration. The sauce boat only returned to favour with the Rococo revival, and from about 1812 until well into the 1820s Rococo-inspired sauce boats and Regency fluted and oak-branch ornamented sauce tureens vied for popular favour, until in the 1830s the Rococo finally took precedence.

A piece of dining-table silver almost entirely restricted to the
28 period under review was the **argyle**. Appearing first in the 1760s, its life was virtually over by 1800, though a few were made in

Pair of sauce tureens and stands, and an argyle or gravy-pot, with bat's wing fluting and gadrooned borders. Richard Carter, Daniel Smith and Robert Sharp. 1785. 97 oz. Private collection. (Mark: see 63).

One of a set of four entrée dishes with shaped gadrooned and foliate borders.
Craddock & Reid. 1813. The set 254 oz. Private collection.

the first few years of the 19th century. The argyle was symp-
tomatic of the new interest in gadgets, which exercised the brains
of many inventors and produced, among other things, telescopic
travelling candlesticks and various coffee percolators. The
purpose of the argyle was to keep the gravy hot, usually by
means of a hot iron placed in a central aperture or in the base, or
by hot water poured into a special compartment within or around
the gravy container. Adam classicism converted the original
cylindrical shape into the ubiquitous vase, with a long curved
spout and a wooden handle either opposite or at right angles to
the spout. Variations were the egg-shaped and the bell-shaped
argyles.

It was not easy to change the fashion of dishes and plates, and
the Neo-classical version differed little from its predecessors,
though pearled and reeded, or reed-and-tie, borders provided a
more formal appearance. The new century saw a return, or rather
greater use, of the gadroon and the shaped gadroon border,
sometimes with shell or foliate motifs at intervals.

29, 30   Much the same applied to the design of the **entrée** and other
31   **serving dishes**, which were often persistently plain even during

the early 1800s. Only then did some rather splendid deep entrée dishes begin to appear, with high domed and fluted covers, enriched with foliate handles. In the years of the Regency proper, from 1811 onwards, friezes of honeysuckle and foliage scrolls and the increased use of applied masks, foliage and so on added to the magnificence of the dinner service in the last years of its greatness.

A few dishes for special purposes also made their début in the 1770s, notably the **toasted cheese dish**, with trays for cheese and a hot water compartment below. About 1800 came the soufflé dish in silver, with either a silver or a plated liner. The pierced oval or circular mazarine, or fish straining dish, made to fit over the well of a large dish, changed little from its Rococo predecessors, except perhaps to feature rather formal geometrical piercing, while the dish cross and lamp and the chafing dish conformed to Neo-classicism only by becoming slightly formal in the treatment of the pierced supports.

31

One of a set of four entrée dishes with high fluted covers.
Paul Storr. 1817. Width 11½ in. The set 357·5 oz. Private collection.

Toasted cheese dish.
John Moore. 1804. Width $9\frac{1}{2}$ in. 59·5 oz. Private collection.

Casserole and cover, made for the actress Sarah Siddons.
Robert Sharp. 1797. Diameter $7\frac{3}{4}$ in. 32·8 oz. Private collection.

One of a pair of 'skep' honey pots and stands with bee finial.
John, Henry and Charles Lias. 1830.
The pair 44·2 oz.
Private collection.

One of a set of four Regency salts on plinths.
Benjamin and James Smith. 1810.
The set 73·9 oz. Formerly in the collection of Lord Howe.

Sugar caster. John Delmester. 1773.
Height 5¾ in. Private collection.

Mustard pot with blue glass liner. William Abdy. 1786. Height 5¼ in. Private collection.

32, 33   **Salts** and **casters** had often, from quite early in the 18th century, been the work of specialist silversmiths who made little else. Some continued to make sugar and pepper casters of traditional
32, 34   **baluster form,** but many now turned their attention to **cruets,** most of them by the 1780s fitted with silver-mounted glass bottles. The classical oval was interpreted by the boat-shaped stand, either with a pierced gallery to enclose the bottles, as in the one by Hester Bateman dated 1788 in the Victoria and Albert Museum, or with ring frames, such as the one of the following year by John Schofield in the same museum. The oval was dropped, of course, early in the 1800s, and the frame stand became heavier in appearance, often unpierced and with bulging sides, until again the Rococo revival brought back the intricate piercing and cinquefoil pattern of the earlier Warwick cruet.

        Piercing found a place early in the 1770s for both salts and
32   **mustard pots.** Probably the best known of all salt makers were the Hennells, who soon adapted their Rococo piercing to the

One from a set of six boat-shaped salts with reeded rims and handles.
Solomon Hougham. 1802. Private collection. (Mark: see 61).

formal vertical slits and overlaid festoons required by the Neo-classicists for the frames of the blue glass ovals and drums for salts and mustards.

Boat-shaped, miniature unlidded versions of the sauce tureen kept abreast with changing dinner service styles, gradually becoming more decorative as the century ended. Even the humble salt could not. avoid, however, the grander themes of the Regency; they became larger and were set proudly on tripod pedestals or stands, with chased bellied bodies and applied lions'

Boat-shaped toast rack with reeded handles.
Burrage Davenport. 1784. Length 10 in. 9·7 oz. Private collection.

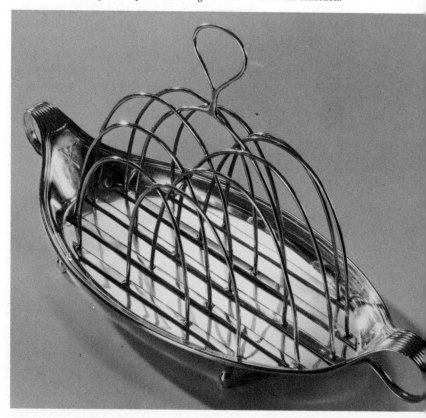

masks that in themselves seemed restrained twenty years later, when the Rococo revivalists found inspiration for the service of salt in kneeling negroes, snaky and rocky bases and tritons blowing conches.

For mustard the plain drum remained the most practical form, and glass liners protected the silver from corrosion. The nearest that the classicists of the 1800s could get to the classical for mustards was the sarcophagus, a short-lived fashion to which the plain drum never, in fact, bowed.

Boat-shaped cruet with silver mounted cut glass bottles.
Paul Storr. 1799. Length 15 in. Private collection.

Silver for the breakfast table was also made in large quantities. Besides bacon and other dishes for hot food, there were silver egg-boilers, sometimes with egg-timers perched above the cover, egg-cup frames and combined egg-cup and cruet frames, toast racks, honey pots, preserve dishes, shell dishes for butter and 34 other table necessities. **Toast racks** were almost an invention of the Adam period, and the oval was usual, with detachable wirework divisions, until the advent of the oblong fixed bar type at the beginning of the 19th century, when of course heavier floral and foliate moulded borders superseded the more delicate-looking beading and reeding of the age of Adam.

32 The age also saw the fashion for beehive or **'skep' honeypots**, which appeared about 1790 and continued in favour until about 1830. Most were simply silver models of the straw beehive placed over a glass honey jar, but some were formed as pots 32 themselves, with the upper part detachable as a lid. **Bee finials** were usual, though sometimes flower or other finials were made. Other jams and preserves were accommodated in silver mounted cut glass pots, sometimes on stands.

Butter shells followed the styles of the earlier Rococo period, imitating scallop shells encrusted often with winkle and other natural pattern feet and with the ribs of the shell matted and polished.

Typically Regency Coburg pattern flatware. About 1820. Private collection.

The basis of early Neo-classical flatware was the Old English pattern, which about 1760 had begun to replace the slightly more slender Hanoverian. It was either left plain, or ornamented along

37 the edges with beading, **feather-edge** – a deep curved cut – or a threaded edge. Tea-table and dessert flatware was often engraved by the bright-cut technique with a variety of charming husk and festoon motifs. The more decorative styles came earlier to flatware than to hollow-wares in general, and the now ubiquitous fiddle pattern was popularised about 1790. Sometimes plain, more often decorated with shells, honeysuckle and other classical motifs, it formed the basis for a host of patterns, including King's, Queen's, Prince's, hour-glass, and fiddle, thread and shell, which held sway throughout the rest of the period. But even these were not elaborate enough for the lovers of finery,

36 and such intricate designs as **Coburg** and pierced vine added their weight to the variety of designs that were turned out by the makers in London, Birmingham and, most of all, Sheffield.

The most elaborate flatware patterns were those devoted to dessert services, and it is not surprising that throughout the period, even when taste veered towards plainness, fruit and

39, 38 **cake baskets, dessert stands** and plates, sweetmeat baskets and centrepieces should all have shown rather more decoration than silver for savouries. Indeed Adam designs did not manage to

Feather-edge flatware. About 1780. Private collection.

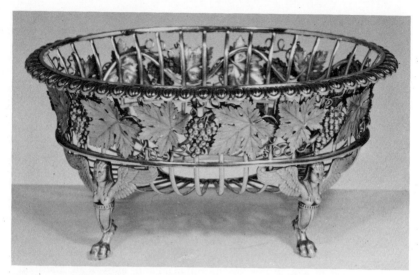

One of a pair of dessert baskets with applied vine decoration and sphinx-and-paw feet. Paul Storr. 1815. Width 12½ in. Private collection.

Dessert basket and stand. John Wakelin and William Taylor. 1784. Private collection.

capture the makers of baskets and **épergnes** in general until about 1776 – some years after their success in every other field of silversmithing.

The table basket, for cake, fruits or sweetmeats, was, of course, oval, and, except for a few unusual baskets and stands by Wakelin & Taylor in the 1780s, generally stood on an oval foot. The sides were splayed, and if pierced, then the piercing was usually vertical, and perhaps mounted with applied festoons and drapes.

Cake basket with Greek key border and beading.
Hester Bateman. 1779. Width 12¾ in. 23·3 oz. Private collection.

Many plainer baskets featured less piercing, perhaps restricting it to a few pierced flowerheads and a border of scrolls or slits, and replacing the overall piercing with swags and borders of bright-cut engraving.

The épergne or centrepiece with its arms suspending baskets and dishes relied on the boat-shape and vertical piercing overlaid with festoons for its classical appeal, the central dish often further accentuating its classicism by two high loop handles.

From about 1800 onwards, the central basket of the épergne and the single cake basket were almost interchangeable, with

Classical oval épergne. Robert Hennell. 1787.
Height overall 18¼ in. 84·2 oz. Private collection.

openwork wire sides and now often circular in outline. The épergne no longer extended four or eight branches, but often had only two, or was transformed into a massive and important centrepiece flanked by two smaller versions of itself down the length of the table. Like the candelabrum, the **dessert centre-**

41 **piece** was largely influenced by the classical caryatid arranged in threes on a triangular plinth to support the regal basket on their heads. Sometimes heavily cut glass bowls replaced the silver or silver-gilt baskets (many centrepieces were gilt) while in time even more elaborate and less formal figure themes were used.

Dessert basket centrepiece supported by three caryatids on a double tripod plinth. Paul Storr. 1812. Height 13 in. 123·9 oz. Private collection.

Goblet, gilt inside. Prince & Co., York. 1805. Height 6 in. 11·3 oz. Private collection. (Mark: see 62).

For serving desserts and cakes richly bordered footed salvers became fashionable about 1803, and very richly pierced vine and grape borders, sometimes enclosing tiny cupids, masks and scrolls, added to the already often richly chased centres, which might contain a coat of arms within a floral design or which might be fluted into a central wreath enclosing the armorials.

Salvers (handleless trays), for carrying anything from a complete meal to a letter, were made in all sizes. Adam ones were usually plain, oval or circular, and with little ornament other than bright-cut engraved borders. Richness came with the new century, and elaborate shaped borders, applied with cast and pierced work of a superb quality, decorated salvers that must have, by their very massiveness, made many a footman groan beneath their weight.

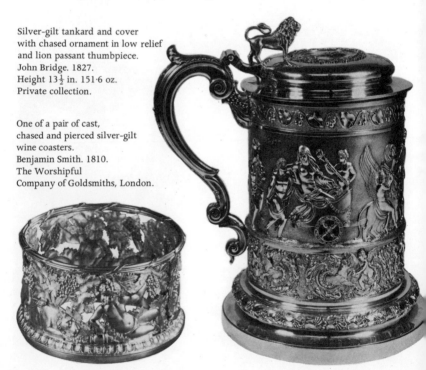

Silver-gilt tankard and cover
with chased ornament in low relief
and lion passant thumbpiece.
John Bridge. 1827.
Height $13\frac{1}{2}$ in. 151·6 oz.
Private collection.

One of a pair of cast,
chased and pierced silver-gilt
wine coasters.
Benjamin Smith. 1810.
The Worshipful
Company of Goldsmiths, London.

Perhaps the most typical item of silver in the Regency strong-room was the **wine cooler.** Though not, of course, unknown before the 1790s, it was by then firmly established and was supplied in pairs, fours and even dozens by the fashionable silversmiths of the period. The classical vase-shape might almost have been designed with the winebottle in mind, and it appeared as the basic form, with differing degrees of ornament, until the 1830s. Even the Rococo revivalists retained the compana- or bell-shape, with its everted lip and slightly bulging base to the shaped body, which was a superb field for every species of classical or Neo-classical ornament and for the 'bas-relief' scenes from classical myth and story devised by Flaxman and his ilk.

Bottle stands and decanter stands – usually known as **wine-coasters** – were frequent drinking companions from the 1770s

One of a set of four wine coolers of classical vase form.
Digby Scott and Benjamin Smith for Rundell, Bridge & Rundell. 1806.
Height 11 in. The set 512 oz. Private collection.

One of a pair of silver-gilt wine coolers.
Robert Garrard. 1816.
Height 10½ in. The pair 195 oz.
Private collection.

onwards. Early Adam styles were often pierced around the sides or were engraved with bright-cut festoons and borders. Occasionally double coasters are found, a pair of sockets being fitted in a boat-shaped stand; but most wine coasters were simple circular stands, often with wooden bases.

A deeper version with elaborate vine and grape pierced sides made its appearance on the tables of the wealthy about 1804, and many variations of these cast and pierced and chased styles were made, alongside the more plebeian plain or fluted versions.

Tankards and mugs were not generally considered part of the elegant furnishing of the dining saloon. Those that were made probably mostly as christening presents, were usually barrel-shaped or slightly tapered, and frequently decorated with row upon row of reeding. Only about 1820 was the covered tankard of any size revived, when it was considered a suitable piece of plate to give as a race prize, and a number of large and highly elaborate **silver-gilt tankards** were made.

The footed wine cup, on the other hand, was made not only for presentation but also, apparently, for use at table, particularly, in the years up to about 1810, while, in the provinces especially, such **goblets** maintained their popularity even later.

Punch remained a popular drink in Britain, but the silver **punch bowl** gradually vanished from the silversmith's shelves. The most notable punch bowls of the period are those given as race prizes at Chester, of which several have been recorded and which generally conformed to the bombé form (with swelling sides) actually seen on the race cards of the 1770s.

A whole group of other silverwares were also pressed into the service of the drinker – wine labels, which from the 1770s onwards assumed most varied forms, from plain oblongs and crescents to elaborate escutcheons, and later developed into cast and chased shells, vine leaves and other elaborate vinous themes; wine funnels, used for straining wines into decanters and usually made in two parts – a round perforated strainer section mounted on a curved funnel; and brandy saucepans, or pannicans, usually baluster in form, though sometimes with tapered sides.

Saucepans of all shapes and sizes were in fact made in large numbers, and the grander versions, like pie-dishes and other silver for the kitchen, must indeed have been used for cooking. Survivals of an earlier age were table wares such as marrow scoops, for getting the marrow out of large bones, nutmeg graters – almost personal silver as they were often carried in the pocket – nutcrackers and other small items. Grape scissors during the first quarter of the 19th century were often chased with suitably vine-decked subjects, while all sorts of new-fangled items such as ice-spoons and meat grippers helped to make the late Georgian table groan beneath a weight of glittering and splendid silver.

Punch bowl with applied acanthus and floral festoons.
Daniel Smith and Robert Sharp. 1779. Height 11¼ in. 120 oz. Private collection.

Silver for the Tea Ceremony

The etiquette of tea-taking at court during the period meant the strict observance of rules for preparing the drink. Fanny Burney, the diarist, noted in 1785 that tea was brought to the King 'upon a large salver, containing sugar, cream, and bread and butter, and cake'. By now, indeed, matching silver tea services were becoming the rule rather than the exception.

The Adam style vase was quickly adopted by the most fashionable hostesses, and one of the earliest services in the new style was a **set of 1774** by James Young and Orlando Jackson, belonging to the actor David Garrick. The set comprises seven pieces – teapot, urn, hot water jug, hot milk jug, cream jug and a pair of basins. The jugs are vase-shaped, but the silversmiths still seemed unsure of how best to interpret the Neo-classical for the teapot, urn and baskets, all of which are hemispherical. Complete unity is given the set, however, by the matted and plain vertical stripes, apparently imitating Wedgwood's jasperware. Festooned drapes and small flowerheads break the line of urn, large jug and teapot, while formal leaf borders and laurel wreaths enclosing the arms of Garrick and his wife show how Adam themes were readily used to good advantage on silver.

A good many tea services were assembled, rather than purchased as sets, which are rarer and, when found, usually of the best workmanship. But tea drinking was the universal social pastime from one end of the country to the other, and in fact was also an increasing, albeit somewhat costly, habit among the work-

47

ing classes and even the very poor. Writing of the people of Nottingham in the middle years of the century, Charles Deering noted: 'The People here are not without their Tea, Coffee and Chocolate, especially the first, the Use of which is spread to that Degree, that not only the Gentry and Wealthy Traders drink it constantly, but almost every Seamer, Sizer and Winder will have her Tea and will enjoy herself over it in a Morning . . .'

With tea so popular, tea silver of every kind was much sought after by those who could afford it. About 1780 the drum-shaped

Tea service with vertical matting, formerly owned by David Garrick.
James Young and Orlando Jackson. 1774. 181·5 oz.

teapot was firmly established as the basic form, to be decorated
49
with every conceivable classical motif. **Andrew Fogelberg**, a
Swede working in London in partnership with Stephen Gilbert,
specialised in small applied medallions, cast and chased with
classical figures, scenes and animals in the manner of James
Tassie, who was a gem-cutter living quite near the silversmith's
workshop. Deep borders of Greek key pattern, anthemion (or
honeysuckle), classical foliage, overlapping palm leaves, laurel
swags, formal scrolling borders taken straight from the drawings
of ruined buildings at Baalbek, reeded and beaded edges, drapery
and floral festoons, husks and Vitruvian scrolls all appeared in
the tea-table silver of the 1780s. Applied, chased and bright-cut
engraved ornament were all employed, and the formality of the
designs was further stressed by the straight tapering spouts which
almost entirely superseded the swan-neck spouts of the 1760s.
Occasionally, the teapot was provided with a rounded base and
elevated on a classical stand, enriched with rams' masks and
laurel festoons. But most teapots were provided with simple
salver-like stands to protect the table surface from heat. These
little stands were sometimes wood base, sometimes fitted with
four panel feet and almost always bordered with beading or
reeding.

About 1790 bright-cut engraving was virtually general, and a
prettier form of the oval with fluted angles was extensively used.
Monograms and crests were still enclosed in bright-cut wreaths –
the former suggesting the greater use of silver for tea by middle
class families not entitled to armorials.

49
During the last decade of the century the **straight-sided oval**
began to give way to a more tapered form often decorated with
fluting and slightly incurved towards the cover. Then about 1798
the rectangular and almost circular styles, still usually with flat

top Drum teapot with beaded and bright-cut decoration.
Hester Bateman. 1783. Private collection.

right Circular vase-shaped tea urn on a square plinth.
Paul Storr. 1821. Height 15 in. 157·25 oz. Private collection.

far right Cream jug with Vitruvian scroll and applied medallion.
Andrew Fogelberg and Stephen Gilbert. 1780. Private collection.

bases, though occasionally on a rim foot, were introduced. Within
the next year or two **high upswept collars** began to enclose the
very slightly domed covers, as in an oval pot of 1798 by Jonathan
Allen in the Victoria and Albert Museum.

By the Regency period the teapot was frequently of a compressed shape on four cast paw feet or, in simpler versions, on ball feet. Gadrooned edges and half-fluting up the bodies became general, and the spout was usually fairly short and curved. One or two pots were very highly decorated. As early as 1803 Digby Scott and Benjamin Smith made an elaborately chased pot with the spout rising to the form of a grouse's head. Within a few years repoussé chasing in the Rococo manner was much used, though Storr and Philip Rundell still tended to use more formal fluted and foliate chased ornament. During the 1820s the melon-shape became firmly established, the panels usually richly chased with scrollwork, flowers and foliage in imitation of the Rococo.

A typical late 18th-century item in the tea service was the urn, which almost without exception replaced the tea-kettle. The urn of course was ideally classical in form, classical vases being copied with superb mastery of detail by silversmiths such as Andrew Fogelberg and Thomas Heming in the 1770s. Early Adam tea-urns were usually tall with short side-handles at the shoulders, with high domed covers and mounted on circular feet raised on square plinths. Almost all the urns of the period had a broad band of classical chasing at the top and were frequently applied with foliate festoons. In the 1780s bright-cut festoons and tall reeded loop handles gave the urn an air of gracious elegance, but within a few years there was a trend towards egg-shaped urns mounted on slender reeded supports, sometimes standing on square or shaped plinths.

The first years of the 19th century saw the **urn** becoming much more pompous, usually circular in form with heavy reeded foliate handles springing from lions' masks, or with ring handles depending from lions' masks. The bodies were hemispherical and nearly always mounted on square plinths. The Rococo revival of the 1820s saw also a revival of the tea-kettle, especially the melon-shaped and inverted pear-shaped forms.

57

49

Even when full tea services were not made, teapot and tea-caddy were often made to match, especially during the 'oval' period. Curiously enough, a chinoiserie style of tea-caddy survived into the Neo-classical period. This was the tea-chest style of caddy with Chinese symbols decorating the sides, which were for the rest chased to suggest wooden tea-chests and were often somewhat incongruously bordered with classical motifs, such as

51 **Greek key** and running scrolls.

The oval quickly came into prominence as the basic form of the

2 **tea-caddy.** Beautiful and fine engraving, often bright-cut, gave the decoration of caddies a crisp and delicate appearance, further enhanced by the decorated chests, in fishskin, tortoiseshell, ivory, mother-of-pearl and all manner of rich woods. Caddies and sugar boxes fitting into chests were sometimes more conveniently designed as oblongs, but many individual caddies appeared in attractively shaped versions of the oval, with fluted angles and elegant festoons of engraving.

There was a certain adherence to the classical urn form for some caddies and sugar vases, but their not very practical shape rather limited their appeal at the tea-table, and the octagonal, oval and oblong dominated tea-caddy form until about 1800, when the oval tended to disappear and the oblong proved itself the most popular. By then a new economical style of caddy was much in

Greek key
(see 39)

Covered silver-gilt sugar vase from the Duke of Wellington's ambassadorial service (1814). Benjamin and James Smith 1810. Height 8 in. Victoria and Albert Museum (Apsley House), London.

Pierced sugar basket with blue glass liner. Maker's mark: IH, II. Newcastle. 1774. Private collection.

use – with two divisions, one for green tea, one for black, instead of having two separate caddies from which to blend the teas.

The imposing Regency style rather overlooked the caddy. A rare caddy of 1818, made by Emes and Barnard for Rundell, Bridge & Rundell, took the form of an oblong octagonal casket heavy with gadroon mounts and on claw and honeysuckle feet. But, except for elaborate caddies made during the Rococo revival of the 1820s, the day of the tea-caddy in silver was virtually over.

52   **Sugar bowls** at the beginning of the Adam period were frequently pierced and fitted with blue glass liners. The pierced style had been popular during the 1760s, and the Adam style merely altered the piercing, bringing formality with vertical slits and overlaid foliate festoons. Almost identical swing handled pails of this type were used for cream, but by the 1780s the two types diverged again, and sugar baskets followed the pattern of

Typical Regency tea service with double snake handles.
Paul Storr. 1815. 133 oz. Private collection.

sweetmeat baskets and became oval, mounted on an oval stepped
foot and with a swing handle from side to side.

When the oval was banished in the early 1800s, silversmiths
began to produce richly decorated covered vases for sugar. From
52   about 1805 onwards there was a series of covered **sugar 'urns'**
with short side-handles and circular dish-like plinths on elaborate
feet. These were first made by Digby Scott and Benjamin Smith –
a set made by Benjamin and James Smith in 1810 was included in
the Duke of Wellington's ambassadorial service – and were later
repeated in 1814 by Paul Storr, for a set of four formerly at Hare-
wood House. In general, however, the sugar bowl was wholly
part of the tea services of the period, usually circular, sometimes
bombé and often half-fluted. Handles on either side were frequently highly ornamental – Paul Storr, for one, had a liking for
53, 59   **intertwined snakes** on the more important items in his tea ser-

vices. Scroll handles gradually returned and were almost standard by the 1820s, when decoration also ruled the rest of the tea equipage.

49, 55 The cream pail with its blue glass liner was generally replaced about 1780 by the **jug**. A few were made of classical vase form, but presumably the difficulty of keeping them clean led to their being superseded by the simpler helmet shape, sometimes mounted on a square or shaped pedestal foot. About 1800,

Tea and coffee service with typical Regency classical motifs, including sphinx-and-paw feet. John Emes. 1805 and 1806. 221·4 oz. Private collection.

however, squatter styles began to come in, following the outline of the teapot and the sugar bowl, and sometimes even with short spouts so that they looked like miniature unlidded teapots. More often, however, the compressed circular shape of the pots was 53, 54 simply repeated and the milk or **cream jug** simply supplied with a broad lip for easy pouring.

One effect of the Neo-classical taste for the vase-shape, added to the swing from coffee and chocolate to tea, was the gradual dis-

Cream jug. Francis Crump. 1773. Height 5½ in. Private collection.

Typically Adam-style vase-shaped coffee jug. Daniel Smith and Robert Sharp. 1774. Height 12½ in. 45 oz. Private collection.

appearance of the coffee pot as such. Indeed, many **jugs** of the period can indiscriminately be described as hot water jugs, coffee pots, chocolate jugs and even ewers.

The **Adam urn or vase** was a most attractive, though perhaps not a very practical form of jug. The natural shoulder above the egg-shaped body was often beautifully chased with husks, acanthus foliage or other formal borders; the base of the body might be chased with overlaid foliage, or applied with, say, eight large and bold palm-leaf straps. The long narrow neck would sometimes be left plain, and sometimes it was fluted. Above the decoration round the base might be hung applied festoons, perhaps caught up with medallions, flowerheads or grinning satyr masks. Beaded edges gave strength to the rims with their short everted lips, while graceful loop handles, at times wicker-bound for better insulation, had a graceful air. While the usual style of foot was circular and then mounted on a sturdy square pedestal, a few jugs of the 1770s followed classical wine jug forms and were mounted with slender curved legs on to triangular pedestals, as on a superb chocolate jug of 1777 by Henry Green-way in the Victoria and Albert Museum.

In plainer form, relieved only with typical bright-cut engrav-ing, the tall covered jug continued the use of the urn-shape right up to the end of the century. One or two variants crept in, how-ever. Some were elongated versions of the traditional baluster jug, used for the past half century or so for wine and beer jugs. Others followed the fluted ovals of the teapot, merely being made taller and given a high shaped foot and curvaceous spout. Some even followed pottery originals, while at the very end of the century new patented inventions for making coffee brought in the straight-sided filter pot known after its inventor as the biggin. These biggins, as well as most hot water jugs of the turn of the century, were fitted with lamps and stands. Paul Storr was pre-eminent with a revival at this period of the classical urn-shape for such jugs. The bodies were a little less elongated, the necks much broader, and most were decorated with narrow formal bands of applied chased wire below the handle socket at the top, which often took the form of a female classical mask, while the lower end terminated in a scroll and formal flowerhead, or perhaps even a double snake. The stand was bordered to match and usually had pendant ring handles and three paw feet below applied formal foliage. These were typical Storr designs, and lesser silversmiths and customers of moderate means were generally content with tall versions of the teapot for the jugs that held either the breakfast coffee or the tea-table hot water, as one wished.

Since in every house, large or small, drinking tea was so important a social occasion, those who could purchased a large tea tray on which to assemble the tea service and the china needed for the ceremony. Oval tea trays, with end-handles, dominate the silver scene throughout the period, although many changing styles of decoration, from nothing but a reeded, beaded or pierced border, to broad bands of engraving and, later, flat chasing and heavy cast and chased rims, succeeded one another.

As the decoration varied, so did the size and weight of the

Compressed half-fluted tea and coffee service.
Philip Rundell. 1821. 120 oz. Private collection.

trays; some of them were scarcely portable at all. Smaller trays measured from 18 to about 22 inches long, but the larger versions might be as much as 28 or 30 inches from handle to handle. A small tray might weigh as little as 40 ounces, or as much as 100 ounces, while the more usual sizes, something over two feet long, often weighed 150 ounces, and exceptionally large ones over 31 inches long might be well over 250 ounces.

Decorated trays until about 1805 were almost all ornamented with bright-cut engraving, generally in a broad border below the rim and with a suitably classical surround for the owner's coat of arms. After that, tremendously intricate and heavy borders were chosen by all who could afford them – among them the Duke of Cumberland, who in 1805 had a tray made by Digby Scott and Benjamin Smith. Weighing over 250 ounces and measuring $25\frac{3}{4}$ inches across, the tray has an intricate sloping border of heavy

Large tray presented to Capability Brown by Cambridge University. John Wakelin and William Taylor. 1780. Width $23\frac{3}{4}$ in. 118 oz. Private collection.

grape clusters and vine-leaves in openwork design. Grand handles have leopards' mask centres and terminate on either side in cornucopias. The inner border of the tray has a deep band of scrolling foliage, while the centre is beautifully engraved with the arms and supporters of the Duke. Elaborate cast detail even forms the feet, enriched with bacchante masks and stags' legs. Oval trays of the period generally became rather more elaborate: the borders were usually moulded and enriched with acanthus motifs at intervals, while handles sprang from highly decorated mounts. Oblongs began to take over from the oval, and occasionally circular trays were made. By the 1820s borders were rich and heavy, with grapevine themes very much to the fore, and shells, scrolls, heavy gadrooning and foliage in evidence elsewhere. A number of **important trays** were gilt, suggesting their use secondarily as sideboard ornaments.

Silver-gilt tray with elaborate cast, chased and pierced border.
Philip Rundell. 1822. Width 22½ in. 158·5 oz. Private collection.

Changes in the Hallmarks 1770-1830

The slow but readily identifiable changes in the design of silver make it possible to hazard accurate guesses at the date of even unmarked silver. It is, in fact, always good practice to look at a piece of silver first of all without reference to the hallmarks. The feel of a piece, its general appearance and the style of any engraved armorials or inscription should be taken into account. Confirmation (or rejection!) of one's surmise when the marks are examined goes a long way to building up a sound knowledge of English silver styles.

Except for certain small articles, nearly all silver of the period is fully hallmarked – that is, it bears a maker's mark, a town mark, the standard mark and the date letter. After 1784, the king's head duty mark was also struck. From about 1780 onwards even many small and hitherto exempted articles were hallmarked, especially at Birmingham.

Paul Storr

THE MAKER'S MARK. The maker's mark continued to take the form of the maker's initials, or the initials of a partnership or company. The mark had to be registered at the assay office (or offices) to which the silversmith or firm sent wares for assay (or testing), and each piece was struck with the maker's mark before it was sent for assay.

THE ASSAY OFFICE MARKS. Each assay office has its own mark, and when the silver has been tested and passed as of the correct standard, the office stamps its own mark, together with the standard mark, date letter and any other statutory mark. During this period the following English assay offices were functioning: London, Chester, Exeter, Newcastle and York. From 1773 onwards there were Birmingham and Sheffield also, offices set up largely due to the efforts of the Birmingham industrialist, Matthew Boulton. Birmingham and Sheffield had for some years been greatly extending their output of silver and plate. The silver had, of course, to be sent to an assay office to be marked. Chester, Newcastle and London were all too far away for either safety or speed, and finally in 1773, despite bitter opposition, offices were established in both cities by Act of Parliament.

London
mark on
salts
(see 33)

LONDON. London uses the mark of a leopard's head. This appeared with a crown until the assay year which began at the end of May 1821, since when it has been uncrowned.

BIRMINGHAM. The mark assigned to the new office at Birmingham in 1773 was an anchor.

CHESTER. Until 1779 the Chester town mark was the three lions of England dimidiating the three garbs (or wheatsheaves) of the Earldom of Chester. From 1779 the simpler Chester mark of three garbs with a sword between in a plain shield were used. Chester also added the London leopard's head mark, crowned until 1823, but uncrowned after then.

EXETER. The Exeter town mark is a triple-towered castle. Until 1777 the leopard's head crowned mark was also used on Exeter silver.

NEWCASTLE. The triple castle of Newcastle is arranged with two towers above a single tower. Newcastle also added the leopard's head crowned and continued to use it crowned up to 1846.

Sheffield
mark on
candlesticks
(see 16
top right)

SHEFFIELD. A crown was prescribed as the town mark of the Sheffield assay office on its foundation in 1773. In many instances from 1780 onwards the crown is found above or at the side of the date letter, chiefly on small silverwares.

York mark
on goblet
(see 41)

YORK. The assay office at York was closed from 1717 until shortly after 1773, and very little plate was assayed there until the 1780s. The town mark is a cross charged with five lions passant, and the leopard's head crowned was also used throughout the period, although marking was somewhat sporadic at York at this period.

THE STANDARD MARK. The minimum standard of silver permitted in England is known as the sterling standard. It is 925 parts per 1000 pure silver (pure silver is too soft for general use), and is denoted by the punch of the lion passant (standing facing left). Only one other standard is allowed, the higher standard of 958 parts pure silver, which is marked with two special marks – the lion's head erased and the figure of Britannia (hence the name 'Britannia standard') – used in place of the leopard's head crowned and the lion passant.

1796
(London)

THE DATE LETTER. Each assay office has its own cycle of date letters. The style of the letter and the shape of the shield are usually changed with each cycle and, except for Sheffield from 1773 to 1823, are arranged in alphabetical order. The London date letter cycles cover twenty years, omitting J and V to Z inclusive. As the first year of each office's cycle and the style and length of the series used vary, it is advisable to consult published tables of date letters.

Marks including incuse duty mark on tureen tray (see 28)

THE DUTY MARK. In 1784 it was decreed that a mark showing the sovereign's head in profile should be used to denote that duty had been paid on all wrought silver. It was imposed on 1st December 1784 and remained in force until 1890. In 1784 and 1785 the duty mark took the form of the King's head facing left and incuse in a square with cut corners. After that, it was struck in cameo, facing right. Various versions were used at the different offices, presumably as the punches became worn.

THE DUTY DRAWBACK MARK. One of the rarest marks on English silver is the figure of Britannia standing, an incuse mark struck on exported plate exempted from duty for only nine months in 1784–1785. Its use was terminated after representations that the application of the mark after the wares were finished damaged the silver. It is, however, occasionally met with on pieces that have returned from overseas.

In reading hallmarks, it is essential to take into account not only the various marks used, but the style of the marks and the shape of the shields in which they are enclosed. This is, for instance, of especial importance when reading marks for London when the town mark is omitted, as on many small objects and on much flatware (spoons and forks). The cycles of date letters in 1776–1795 and 1816–1835 were identical, so special note must be taken of the duty mark and the form of the lion passant.

Acknowledgements

Photographs (or the object for photographing) were kindly made available by
Asprey & Co. Ltd, London; J.H. Bourdon-Smith Ltd, London; Bracher & Sydenham
Ltd, Reading; Christie, Manson & Woods Ltd, London; T.Lumley, Esq.; S.J.
Shrubsole Ltd, London; Sotheby & Co. Ltd, London; C.J. Vander (Antiques) Ltd,
London.
The photographs on pages 23 top, 28, 32 left and bottom right, 36, 37, 49 top and
55 left were specially taken by Peter Parkinson AIBP.

COUNTRY LIFE COLLECTORS' GUIDES

Series editor Hugh Newbury
Series designer Ian Muggeridge

Published for Country Life Books by
THE HAMLYN PUBLISHING GROUP LIMITED
LONDON · NEW YORK · SYDNEY · TORONTO
Hamlyn House, Feltham, Middlesex, England

LATE GEORGIAN AND REGENCY SILVER
ISBN 0 600 43203 3
© The Hamlyn Publishing Group Limited 1971
Printed by Toppan Printing Co. (H.K.) Limited, Hong Kong